SALADS & SNACKS

Edited by
Rhona Newman

Contents

This edition first published 1979 by
Octopus Books Limited
59 Grosvenor Street, London W.1.

© 1979 Octopus Books Limited

ISBN 0 7064 1014 9

Produced and printed in Hong Kong by
Mandarin Publishers Limited
22a Westlands Road, Quarry Bay

Frontispiece: SAVOURY STUFFED TOMATOES *(page 90)*
(Photograph: Taunton Cider Kitchen)

Weights and Measures

All measurements in this book are based on Imperial weights and measures, with American equivalents given in parenthesis.

Measurements in *weight* in the Imperial and American system are the same. Liquid measurements are different, and the following table shows the equivalents:

Liquid measurements
1 Imperial pint .... 20 fluid ounces
1 American pint .... 16 fluid ounces
1 American cup .... 8 fluid ounces

Level spoon measurements are used in all the recipes.

Spoon measurements
1 tablespoon (1T) .... 15 ml
1 teaspoon .... 5 ml

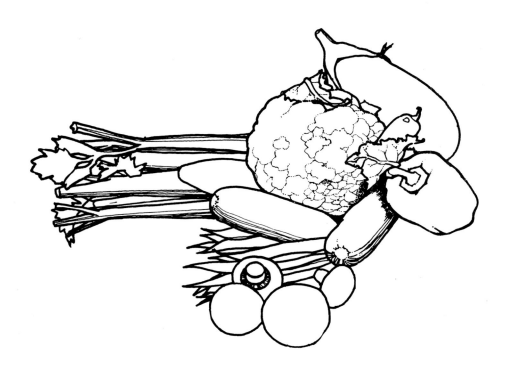

INTRODUCTION

If the very word 'salads' conjures up visions of limp lettuce leaves, half a tomato and a few slices of cucumber, and 'snacks' suggests beans on toast or a ham sandwich, just glance through the pages of delicious recipes in this exciting and colourful cookbook.

'Salads and Snacks' contains a unique collection of appetizing dishes for every meal from a simple picnic to salads for a summer party.

The enterprising cook will find a variety of unusual ideas. For example, try the tangy freshness of citrus fruits or the subtle flavouring of avocado with meat and poultry. Make the most of raw vegetables as the basis for a winter salad and discover the difference in flavour (the vitamins and minerals often lost in cooking will be an added bonus). These versatile dishes may well provide the solution to the perennial problem of planning quick nourishing meals using ingredients from the storecupboard or those leftover vegetables.

Both hot and cold snacks and even the simplest salads can be made more appetizing by the addition of an imaginative garnish. Chopped herbs, tomato slices and crisp lettuce can look very attractive and have the added advantage of being quick and simple to prepare. Here are some additional suggestions you may like to try:

Crimped cucumber: run a fork down the sides of a cucumber, deep enough to remove strips of peel. Slice the cucumber in the usual way.

Cucumber cones: cut thin slices of cucumber and make a cut from the centre to the outer edge. Wrap one cut edge over the other to form a cone.

Radish roses: trim the radishes. Make 4 or 8 small, deep cuts crossing the centre of the root. Place the radishes in cold or iced water for 1 to 2 hours. The cuts will open to form 'petals'.

Celery curls: cut a celery stick into strips about ½ inch wide and 2 inches long. Make cuts along the length of each, close together to within ½ inch of one end. Place in cold or iced water for 1 to 2 hours until the fringed strips curl. Drain well before serving.

Gherkin (dill pickle) fans: use whole long, thin gherkins (dill pickles). Cut lengthwise into thin slices leaving them joined at one end. Arrange the strips so that they fan out and overlap each other.

Tomato lilies: use firm even-sized tomatoes. With a sharp, pointed knife, make a series of V–shaped cuts around the middle of each tomato, cutting right through to the centre. Pull the halves apart carefully.

Lemon and orange twists: cut thin slices of lemon or orange. Make a cut in each slice from the centre to the outer edge. Twist the slice and place in position.

QUICK BAVARIAN PIZZA *(page 58)*
(Photograph: Van den Berghs Ltd.)

MAIN MEAL SALADS

Chef's Summer Salad

2 × ½ inch slices white bread
2 oz. (¼ cup) butter
salt
1 clove garlic
1 head lettuce
1 small onion, cut into thin rings
1 oz. (¼ cup) Parmesan cheese,
  grated
2 oz. (½ cup) button mushrooms,
  sliced

6 oz. (¾ cup) cooked ham, cubed
1 small can anchovy fillets, drained
Dressing:
4 tablespoons (¼ cup) olive oil
1 tablespoon lemon juice
2 tablespoons Worcestershire sauce
salt

Remove the crusts from the bread and cut into ½ inch cubes. Fry in the butter until golden brown on all sides. Drain on paper towels and sprinkle with salt.

Rub a large salad bowl with the cut garlic clove. Tear the lettuce into pieces and place in the bowl. Add the onion, Parmesan cheese, mushrooms, ham and anchovy fillets. Mix well.

Blend the dressing ingredients together. Just before serving pour the dressing over the salad, add the bread cubes and mix well.
Serves 4-6
As an alternative to the ham, try canned salmon or tuna, or cubes of hard cheese such as Cheddar or Emmenthal.

Spiced Egg Salad

8 hard-boiled eggs, quartered
3 green peppers, seeded and
  chopped
1 red pepper, seeded and cut into
  strips
4 button mushrooms, sliced
6 black olives
1 tablespoon chopped walnuts

Dressing:
1 clove garlic, crushed
1 teaspoon paprika pepper
2 tablespoons vinegar
6 tablespoons oil
salt and freshly ground pepper
½ teaspoon sugar

Arrange the eggs, green and red peppers, mushrooms and olives in a salad bowl. Sprinkle the walnuts over the top. In a screw-top jar combine all the dressing ingredients. Shake well and pour the dressing over the salad. Chill for 30 minutes before serving. Serve with crusty rolls and butter.
Serves 4

Egg and Potato Salad Loaf

1½ lb. (4 cups) potatoes, peeled
  and diced
3 hard-boiled eggs, sliced
1 tablespoon (2¼ teaspoons)
  gelatine
2 tablespoons water
3 tablespoons salad cream

1 teaspoon freshly chopped chives
1 small onion, grated
salt and freshly ground pepper
Garnish:
shredded lettuce
parsley sprigs

Line a 2 lb. loaf tin with greaseproof paper (non-stick parchment), so that the paper extends above the top by 2 inches.

Boil the potatoes for about 10 minutes until they are soft but not mushy. Line the loaf tin with the slices of hard-boiled egg. Sprinkle the gelatine onto the water in a heatproof bowl, then place over a pan of gently simmering water and stir until dissolved. Add to the salad cream with the chives, onion and salt and pepper to taste. Mix in the potatoes and spoon into the loaf tin.

Leave until set, then turn onto a serving platter lined with shredded lettuce. Garnish with parsley sprigs.
Serves 6

Chicken, Avocado and Grapefruit Salad

12 oz. (1½ cups) cooked chicken,
 diced
4 oz. (⅔ cup) long-grain rice,
 cooked
2 grapefruit, peeled and segmented
2-3 teaspoons finely chopped onion
2 carrots, peeled and cut into sticks
salt and freshly ground pepper

1 large ripe avocado
2 tablespoons lemon juice
2 tablespoons French dressing
lettuce leaves
watercress to garnish
6 tablespoons mayonnaise
½ teaspoon curry powder

Place the chicken in a bowl with the rice, grapefruit segments, onion, carrots and salt and pepper to taste. Peel and dice the avocado, mix with half the lemon juice and the French dressing. Add to the salad and toss lightly. Arrange the lettuce on a serving platter and pile the salad on top. Garnish with watercress.

Mix the remaining lemon juice with the mayonnaise and curry powder. Spoon over the salad or serve separately.
Serves 4

Hawaiian Chicken Salad

8 oz. (2 cups) macaroni rings
8 oz. (1 cup) cooked chicken,
 chopped
1 stick celery, chopped
1 × 11 oz. can sweetcorn (kernel
 corn), drained
1 × 13 oz. can pineapple, drained

1 tablespoon almonds, blanched
1 large green pepper, seeded and
 chopped
1 tablespoon mayonnaise
2 tablespoons lemon juice
salt and freshly ground pepper
paprika pepper to garnish

Cook the macaroni rings in boiling water for 15–20 minutes, then drain. Mix together the macaroni, chicken, celery, corn, pineapple, almonds and green pepper.

Combine the mayonnaise and lemon juice with salt and pepper to taste. Add the dressing to the chicken mixture and mix thoroughly. Cover the salad and chill for several hours.

Transfer to a serving bowl and sprinkle with paprika pepper.
Serves 4

CHICKEN, AVOCADO AND GRAPEFRUIT SALAD
(Photograph: Carmel Produce Information Bureau)

Italian Chicken with Tuna Sauce

4 chicken portions
1 small onion, halved
1 bay leaf
salt and pepper
½ pint (1¼ cups) chicken stock
1 lb. courgettes (zucchini), thinly sliced

4 tablespoons (¼ cup) French dressing
1 × 3 oz. can tuna fish
½ pint (1¼ cups) mayonnaise
little lemon juice
pimiento strips to garnish

Place the chicken portions in a large pan with the onion, bay leaf, salt and pepper to taste, and the stock. Bring to the boil, cover and simmer for 20 minutes or until tender. Take out the chicken, reserving the stock, and remove the skin when cool enough to handle. Leave until cold. Simmer the courgettes (zucchini) in a little salted water until just tender. Drain thoroughly then toss in French dressing and chill.

Sieve (strain) the tuna fish with its oil, to a purée. Mix with the mayonnaise. Stir in the lemon juice and salt and pepper to taste. The sauce should be thick enough to coat the back of a spoon; if too thick, add a little of the reserved chicken stock.

Arrange the chicken portions on a serving dish, coat with the sauce and garnish with pimiento strips. Chill before serving, with the courgettes (zucchini) arranged around the chicken. A potato salad is an ideal accompaniment to this dish.

Serves 4

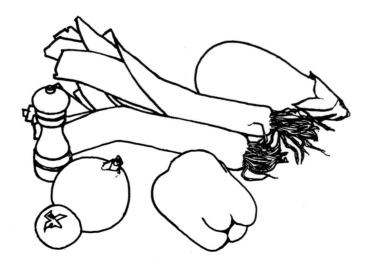

14

Ogen Chicken Salad

1 medium Ogen melon
1 lb. (2 cups) cooked chicken, chopped
1 green pepper, seeded and chopped

4 oz. (1 cup) walnuts, chopped
6 tablespoons mayonnaise
freshly chopped parsley to garnish

Halve the melon and remove the seeds. Scoop out the flesh into balls or cubes. Place in a bowl and add the chicken, green pepper and walnuts. Stir in the mayonnaise and mix well. Serve garnished with chopped parsley.
Serves 4

Winter Salad

4 oz. (½ cup) cooked chicken, diced
8 hard-boiled eggs, quartered
½ small white cabbage, shredded
2 large carrots, grated
4 sticks celery, finely chopped
1 dessert apple, cored and diced
1 tablespoon sultanas (seedless white raisins)

juice of ½ lemon
½ teaspoon curry powder
2 tablespoons double (heavy) cream
½ pint (1¼ cups) mayonnaise
salt and freshly ground pepper
paprika pepper to garnish

Mix the chicken and 6 eggs with the vegetables, apple and sultanas (seedless white raisins) in a large bowl. Beat the lemon juice, curry powder and cream with the mayonnaise. Season to taste with salt and pepper and pour the dressing over the salad. Mix well until all the ingredients are coated. Decorate with the remaining eggs and sprinkle with paprika pepper. Serve with baked potatoes or hot crusty bread.
Serves 4

Minted Melon and Chicken Salad

4 tablespoons (¼ cup) mayonnaise
1 tablespoon lemon juice
salt and freshly ground pepper
pinch of garlic powder (optional)
1 tablespoon freshly chopped chives
2 tablespoons freshly chopped mint

12 oz. (1½ cups) cooked chicken
1 Honeydew melon
lettuce leaves
Garnish:
2 tomatoes
sprig of fresh mint

Mix together the mayonnaise and lemon juice. Season to taste with salt, pepper and garlic powder (if using), then stir in the chives and mint. Cut the chicken into narrow strips and add to the sauce. Halve the melon and remove the seeds. Cut the flesh into cubes or thin slices, add to the salad and mix lightly.

Cover and leave the salad to stand for about 20 minutes before serving. Arrange the lettuce on a serving platter and pile the salad on top. Garnish with tomato wedges and a sprig of fresh mint.
Serves 4

Chicken and Ham Mould

1 tablespoon (2¼ teaspoons)
 gelatine
3 tablespoons water
2 × 15 oz. cans chicken soup
1 teaspoon Worcestershire sauce
salt and freshly ground pepper
1 × 6½ oz. can pimientos, drained
 and chopped

2 oz. (¼ cup) lean ham, cubed
4 oz. (½ cup) cooked chicken,
 chopped
4 inch piece cucumber, cut into
 ½ inch cubes
Garnish:
pimiento strips
cucumber slices

Sprinkle the gelatine over the water in a heatproof bowl, then place over a pan of gently simmering water and stir until dissolved. Mix together the soup, Worcestershire sauce and gelatine mixture. Season to taste with salt and pepper. Add the pimiento, ham, chicken and cucumber. Mix well and pour into a 2 pint (5 cup) mould. Leave to set before turning out onto a serving platter.

Garnish with strips of pimiento and cucumber slices.
Serves 4

MINTED MELON AND CHICKEN SALAD
(Photograph: Carmel Produce Information Bureau)

Cottage Cheese Hawaiian Salad

1 head lettuce
1 head chicory (Belgian endive)
1 × 14 oz. can pineapple rings,
  drained
½ cucumber, sliced
2 large oranges, cut into segments

1 lb. (2 cups) cottage cheese
4 oz. (½ cup) cooked ham,
  chopped
1 teaspoon prepared mustard
3 tablespoons mayonnaise
1 apple, cored and sliced, to garnish

Arrange a bed of lettuce and chicory (Belgian endive) on a serving platter. Place the pineapple rings around it and top with slices of cucumber and a ring of orange segments. Mix the cottage cheese with the chopped ham, mustard and mayonnaise. Spoon into the centre of the salad and garnish with apple slices.
Serves 4

Savoury Cheese Log

8 oz. (2 cups) Cheddar cheese,
  grated
4 hard-boiled eggs, chopped
½ teaspoon prepared mustard
2 teaspoons freshly chopped parsley
2 tablespoons salad cream

2 tablespoons single (light) cream
salt and freshly ground pepper
lettuce leaves
Garnish:
1 tomato, sliced
parsley sprigs

Place the cheese, hard-boiled eggs, mustard and parsley in a bowl. Stir in the salad cream, cream and salt and pepper to taste. Mix well.

  With wet hands, shape the cheese mixture into a roll. Wrap in aluminium foil and place in the refrigerator for 1 hour. When cold and firm, slice the log and arrange on a bed of lettuce. Garnish with tomato slices and parsley sprigs.
Serves 4

Cottage Cheese and Cucumber Mould

1 cucumber
½ teaspoon salt
1 tablespoon sugar
2 tablespoons (4½ teaspoons)
  gelatine

3 tablespoons lemon juice
¼ pint (⅔ cup) hot water
1 lb. (2 cups) cottage cheese
8 fl. oz. (1 cup) mayonnaise
lettuce leaves

Thinly slice half the cucumber and boil gently with the salt and sugar to soften. Strain, keeping ¼ pint (⅔ cup) of the liquid. Dissolve 1 tablespoon (2¼ teaspoons) gelatine in this liquid and add 1 tablespoon lemon juice. Allow to cool.

Place the softened cucumber slices in layers in a ring mould and carefully pour over the gelatine mixture. Refrigerate until set.

Dissolve the remaining gelatine in the hot water and add the remaining lemon juice and a little salt. Leave to cool. Peel and chop the remaining cucumber. Blend the cottage cheese and mayonnaise together. Stir in the cooled gelatine mixture and the chopped cucumber. Pour over the first layer in the ring mould and chill until firm.

Arrange lettuce leaves on a serving platter and turn out the mould.
Serves 6

Cottage Cheese and Peach Salad

8 oz. (2 cups) cottage cheese
3 tablespoons mayonnaise
lettuce leaves
1 fresh peach or canned peaches,
  sliced

Garnish:
8 black grapes or black olives
chopped walnuts

Blend the cottage cheese and mayonnaise together. Arrange lettuce leaves around the edge of a serving dish, and pile the cottage cheese mixture in the centre. Arrange the sliced peaches over the cottage cheese. Garnish with black grapes or black olives and chopped walnuts.
Serves 2

Smoked Mackerel Salad

8 oz. (3 cups) white cabbage,
 shredded
1 large carrot, grated
3 tablespoons mayonnaise
salt and freshly ground pepper

1 head lettuce
4 smoked mackerel fillets, cooked
2 hard-boiled eggs, sliced
watercress to garnish

Mix the cabbage, carrot and mayonnaise together and season to taste
with salt and pepper. Arrange the lettuce leaves around the edge of
an oval serving platter and pile the cabbage and carrot mixture down
the centre. Lay the mackerel fillets over the top and cover each one
with slices of hard-boiled egg. Garnish the dish with sprigs of
watercress.
Serves 4

Smoked Mackerel Niçoise

1 lb. smoked mackerel fillets,
 cooked
8 oz. French (green) beans
8 oz. (2 cups) tomatoes, quartered
½ cucumber, sliced

3 hard-boiled eggs, quartered
12 stuffed green olives
French dressing
freshly chopped parsley to garnish

Skin and cut the smoked mackerel fillets into 1 inch pieces. Cook the
beans, cut in half and leave to cool. Combine all the ingredients,
except the parsley. Toss well to coat in the French dressing.
  Serve in individual bowls garnished with chopped parsley. Serve
with brown or white bread and butter.
Serves 4–6

SMOKED MACKEREL SALAD
(Photograph: The White Fish Kitchen)

Tuna Pasta Salad

4 oz. (1 cup) pasta shapes
1 × 7 oz. can tuna
1 small onion, finely chopped
2 inch piece of cucumber, diced
2 tomatoes, skinned, seeded and
  chopped

4 tablespoons (¼ cup) mayonnaise
grated rind and juice of ½ lemon
salt and freshly ground pepper
lettuce leaves

Cook the pasta in boiling salted water until 'al dente' (just tender to the bite). Drain and rinse in cold water. Drain the tuna and break the fish into large flakes. Mix the fish with the pasta, onion, cucumber and tomatoes.

Blend the mayonnaise with the lemon rind and juice and add to the other ingredients. Mix until evenly coated and add salt and pepper to taste. Arrange some lettuce on a serving platter and pile the pasta mixture into the centre.
Serves 4

Asparagus and Tuna Cream

1 × 15 oz. can green asparagus
1 ½ teaspoons (1 teaspoon) gelatine
¼ pint (⅔ cup) soured cream
2 tablespoons salad cream
1 tablespoon finely chopped onion
salt and freshly ground pepper
2 hard-boiled eggs, chopped

1 × 7 oz. can tuna, drained and
  flaked
Garnish:
shredded lettuce
2 tomatoes, cut into wedges
black olives

Drain the asparagus and reserve 4 tablespoons (¼ cup) of the liquor. Cut each asparagus spear into 3. Sprinkle the gelatine onto the reserved asparagus liquor in a heatproof bowl, then place over a pan of gently simmering water and stir until dissolved.

Mix together the soured cream, salad cream, onion and salt and pepper to taste. Stir in the gelatine and mix well, then fold in the eggs and tuna. Pour into a greased mould and leave to set.

Turn out onto a serving platter and garnish with shredded lettuce, tomatoes and black olives.
Serves 4

Corn Niçoise

1 × 11½ oz. can sweetcorn (kernel
  corn), drained
½ onion, sliced
2 carrots, cut into thin sticks
salt and freshly ground pepper
3 tablespoons French dressing

lettuce leaves
2 heads of chicory (Belgian endive)
1 × 4½ oz. can sardines, drained
Garnish:
cucumber slices
black olives

Place the corn, onion, carrots, salt and pepper and dressing in a bowl
and mix well. Arrange the lettuce leaves and chicory (Belgian endive)
in four individual bowls and spoon the corn mixture into the centre.

Arrange the sardines around the edge and garnish with the
cucumber slices and black olives. Serve with wholemeal
(wholewheat) bread and butter.
Serves 4
Other canned fish, such as tuna, pilchards, salmon or mackerel, can
be used in place of the sardines.

Watermelon Creole

½ watermelon
1 teaspoon curry powder
½ pint (1¼ cups) mayonnaise
2 teaspoons tomato purée (paste)

8 oz. (1⅓ cups) peeled prawns
  (shelled shrimp)
1 green pepper, seeded and chopped
freshly chopped parsley to garnish

Scoop out the flesh of the watermelon discarding the seeds. Scoop
into balls or cut into cubes and reserve some for garnishing. Place the
remainder in a bowl and add the curry powder, mayonnaise, tomato
purée (paste), prawns (shrimp) and green pepper. Mix well and
transfer to a serving bowl or individual dishes.

Garnish with the reserved melon and parsley. Serve with green
salad and brown bread and butter.
Serves 4

Insalata di Funghi (Mushroom Salad)

8 oz. (2 cups) button mushrooms,
  thinly sliced
olive oil
juice of 1 lemon
2 cloves garlic, crushed
6 drops Tabasco sauce
1 teaspoon sugar

salt and freshly ground pepper
8 oz. (1 cup) peeled shrimps
  (shelled shrimp)
¼ pint (⅔ cup) double (heavy)
  cream
lettuce leaves
parsley sprigs to garnish

Place the mushrooms in a bowl, add the oil and leave to soak for 1 hour. Stir in the lemon juice, garlic, Tabasco sauce, sugar and salt and pepper to taste. Just before serving stir in the shrimps and cream.

Arrange lettuce on a serving platter, pile the mushroom salad on top and garnish with parsley. Serve with wholemeal (wholewheat) bread and butter.
Serves 4

Oriental Salad

1 lb. (2 cups) cottage cheese
3 tablespoons double (heavy)
  cream, lightly whipped
4 oz. (½ cup) cooked chicken,
  diced
½ oz. (1T) stem (preserved)
  ginger, finely chopped

Garnish:
lettuce leaves
watercress
tomato wedges

Place all the ingredients in a bowl and mix thoroughly. Pile onto an oval serving dish and garnish with lettuce, watercress and tomato wedges. Serve with wholemeal (wholewheat) bread or rolls.
Serves 4

INSALATA DI FUNGHI
(Photograph: Mushroom Growers' Association)

Lazy Loaf

1 tablespoon (2¼ teaspoons)
  gelatine
¼ pint (⅔ cup) water
½ pint (1¼ cups) stock or soup
12 oz. (1½ cups) cooked meats,
  chopped
salt and freshly ground pepper

pinch of grated nutmeg
pinch of curry powder
Garnish:
1 hard-boiled egg, sliced
radishes
freshly chopped parsley

Sprinkle the gelatine onto the water in a heatproof bowl, then place over a pan of gently simmering water and stir until dissolved.

  Add to the stock or soup and leave to thicken. Season the meat with salt, pepper, nutmeg and curry powder to taste, then add to the stock. Place in a 1 lb. loaf tin and refrigerate until set. Turn onto a serving platter and garnish with slices of hard-boiled egg, radishes and chopped parsley. Serve with a green salad.
Serves 4

Slimmer's Platter

1 head lettuce
4 fresh peaches
1 lb. (2 cups) cottage cheese
8 oz. (1 cup) cooked meat, chopped

1 dessert apple, cored and diced
salt and freshly ground pepper
2 bananas, sliced

Arrange the lettuce on a large serving platter. Peel the peaches, cut into thirds and remove the stones (pits). Mix the cottage cheese with the cooked meat and apple. Season to taste with salt and pepper and pile the mixture onto the lettuce. Arrange the peaches and bananas around the cheese mixture. Serve immediately.
Serves 4

Beef and Orange Rice Salad

4 oz. (½ cup) long-grain rice
1 lb. rump steak
1 oz. (2 T) butter
1 teaspoon salt
2 tablespoons Worcestershire sauce

1 tablespoon water
2 oranges
2 tablespoons oil
1 green pepper, seeded and chopped

Cook the rice in boiling salted water for about 12 minutes until just soft. Rinse with cold water and drain. Cut the rump steak into ¼ inch strips and fry in the butter for about 2 minutes until browned on all sides.

In a large bowl mix the salt, Worcestershire sauce and water together; add the meat and toss to coat in the marinade. Leave for 4 hours turning the meat occasionally.

Grate the rind from 1 orange and set aside. Using a sharp knife, peel both oranges, removing all the white pith, and cut between the sections to remove the segments. Reserve all the juice from the oranges and add to the meat marinade.

Drain the marinade from the meat and mix well with the grated rind and oil. Adjust the seasoning and mix the marinade into the rice with the chopped pepper. Pile the rice onto a serving platter, place the meat strips on top and garnish with the orange segments.
Serves 4

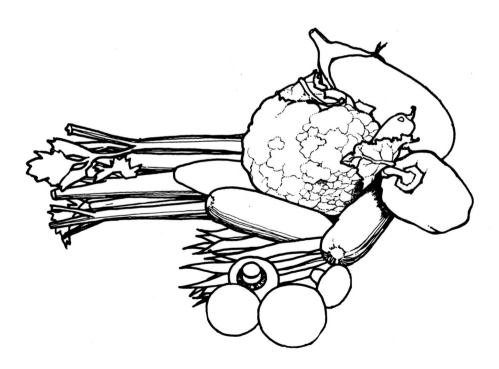

Fresh Fruit Salad

4 oz. (½ cup) sugar
½ pint (1¼ cups) water
juice of ½ lemon
1-2 tablespoons Cointreau liqueur
2 oranges, peeled and segmented

2 bananas, thickly sliced
2 dessert apples, peeled and sliced
2 oz. (½ cup) black grapes, seeded
2 oz. (½ cup) green grapes, seeded
1 pear, peeled and sliced

Make a syrup by dissolving the sugar in the water over a gentle heat.
Bring to the boil for 5 minutes, cool and add the lemon juice and
Cointreau.

Place the prepared fruits in a large bowl and pour the syrup over.
Mix well and leave to stand for 2-3 hours. Transfer to a serving
bowl. If liked, serve with fresh cream or yogurt.
Serves 4
When available, fruits such as melon, pineapple, cherries,
strawberries, raspberries, peaches and apricots can be added to the
fruit salad.

Tangy Harvest Salad

1 lb. small new potatoes, scraped
2 dessert apples, cored and diced
2 sticks celery, chopped
1 pear, cored and diced
8 oz. (1½ cups) cherries, stoned
 (pitted) and halved

4 oz. (½ cup) cottage cheese
8 oz. (2½ cups) Cheddar cheese,
 diced
¼ pint (⅔ cup) soured cream
mint sprigs to garnish

Cook the potatoes in boiling salted water. Drain, cool and cut into
dice. Place in a bowl with the remaining ingredients and mix well.
Turn into a serving bowl and garnish with sprigs of mint. Serve with
a green salad and crusty rolls.
Serves 4

SIDE SALADS

Summer Salad

1 × 11½ oz. can sweetcorn (kernel corn), drained
1 stick celery, chopped

1 large firm tomato, chopped
2 tablespoons French dressing
freshly ground black pepper

Place all the ingredients in a bowl and mix well. Chill, then turn into a serving bowl.
   Serve with hot or cold meats.
Serves 4

Corn and Dill Salad

1 × 11½ oz. can sweetcorn (kernel corn), drained
1 pickled cucumber (dill pickle), sliced

4 oz. (½ cup) long-grain rice, cooked
4 tablespoons (¼ cup) French dressing

Mix all the ingredients together and turn into a serving bowl.
Serves 4–6

Corn and Apple Salad

1 × 11½ oz. can sweetcorn (kernel corn), drained
1 red dessert apple, cored and thinly sliced

1 stick celery, chopped
1 small onion, finely grated
2 tablespoons French dressing

Mix all the ingredients together and turn into a serving bowl. Chill before serving.
Serves 4

Glittering Gold Salad

1 lemon jelly (1 package of lemon-flavored gelatine)
pinch of salt
6 fl. oz. (¾ cup) boiling water
8 fl. oz. (1 cup) cold water

1 tablespoon lemon juice
1 × 7 oz. can sweetcorn (kernel corn), drained
lettuce leaves

Dissolve the jelly (gelatine) and salt in the boiling water. Stir in the cold water and lemon juice. Chill until the mixture begins to set then fold in the corn. Pour into a 1 pint (2½ cup) mould and chill until firm.

Arrange the lettuce on a serving platter and turn the corn mould into the centre.

Serve with cold meats or cheese and crusty rolls.
Serves 4

Mixed Vegetable Salad

2 carrots, cooked and diced
8 oz. (1¼ cups) potatoes, cooked and diced
4 oz. (¾ cup) peas, cooked
4 oz. (½ cup) French (green) beans, cooked and diced

1 × 11½ oz. can sweetcorn (kernel corn), drained
4 tablespoons (¼ cup) mayonnaise
salt and freshly ground pepper

Place the carrots, potatoes, peas, beans and corn in a bowl. Add the mayonnaise and mix well. Season to taste with salt and pepper. Transfer to a serving bowl and chill before serving.
Serves 4
An ideal way of using leftover vegetables.

Potato Salad

1 lb. potatoes, cooked and diced
1/4 pint (2/3 cup) salad cream
salt and freshly ground pepper
1 tablespoon freshly chopped
  parsley
lettuce leaves

Garnish:
black olives
radishes, sliced
watercress sprig

Mix the potatoes with the salad cream, salt and pepper to taste and the chopped parsley. Place lettuce leaves around the edge of a serving bowl and pile the potato into the centre. Garnish with black olives, sliced radishes and a watercress sprig.
Serves 4

Potato Salad Mould

1 tablespoon (2 1/4 teaspoons)
  gelatine
1/4 pint (2/3 cup) hot vegetable stock
6 tablespoons mayonnaise
2 lb. potatoes, cooked and diced

1 × 16 oz. can diced mixed
  vegetables
2 pickled onions, finely chopped
salt and freshly ground pepper

Dissolve the gelatine in the hot vegetable stock. Cool, then add the mayonnaise, stirring thoroughly. Mix in the vegetables and onions and season to taste with salt and pepper.

Place in a 2 1/2 pint (6 1/4 cup) mould and chill until set. Unmould and serve with green salad and cold meats.
Serves 6

Surprise Salad

1 small head (bunch) celery,
  washed and sliced
3 dessert apples, cored and diced
1 bunch radishes, quartered
1 × 10 oz. can mushroom soup

juice of 1/2 lemon
pinch of dry mustard
3 spring onions (scallions), chopped
2 oz. (1/2 cup) mushrooms, sliced
salt and freshly ground pepper

Toss the celery, apples and radishes together. Mix the mushroom soup with the lemon juice, mustard, spring onions (scallions), mushrooms and salt and pepper to taste. Pour over the salad and mix well. Transfer to a serving bowl.
Serves 4

POTATO SALAD
(Photograph: Potato Marketing Board)

Turkish Cucumber Salad

½ medium cucumber
salt
½ pint (1 ¼ cups) natural
  (unflavored) yogurt

1 clove garlic, crushed
1 tablespoon freshly chopped mint
freshly chopped fennel to garnish

Peel the cucumber and slice thinly. Sprinkle with salt and leave for 30 minutes to allow the cucumber to soften. Remove excess salt and drain the cucumber.

Put the yogurt in a bowl and add the garlic, cucumber and chopped mint. Place in a serving dish and sprinkle with fennel.

Serve chilled with curry, fish or grilled meat.

Serves 4–6

Orange and Cucumber Salad

1 × 11 oz. can mandarin oranges
½ cucumber, diced
1 onion, sliced
8 oz. (1 cup) long-grain rice,
  cooked
lettuce leaves

Dressing:
4 fl. oz. (½ cup) corn oil
3 tablespoons reserved orange juice
2 tablespoons lemon juice
salt and freshly ground pepper

Drain the mandarin oranges and reserve the juice. Place the oranges in a bowl with the cucumber, onion and rice. Combine the ingredients for the dressing and pour over the salad. Mix well.

Pile into a serving platter lined with lettuce. Serve chilled.

Serves 4

Mushroom and Bean Salad

6 oz. (1 cup) broad (lima) beans
8 oz. (2 cups) button mushrooms
4 spring onions (scallions)

¼ pint (⅔ cup) natural
  (unflavored) yogurt
salt and freshly ground pepper

Cook the beans in salted water until just tender. Drain and allow to cool. Wipe the mushrooms and slice thinly. Chop the onions (scallions) and mix in a bowl with the beans and mushrooms. Stir in the yogurt and season to taste with salt and pepper.

Serve with cold meats, hard-boiled eggs or canned fish.

Serves 4

Pepper and Mushroom Salad

1 small green pepper, seeded
1 small red pepper, seeded
8 oz. (2 cups) mushrooms, sliced
3 sticks celery, sliced
1 onion, finely chopped

Dressing:
6 tablespoons vegetable oil
2 tablespoons white wine vinegar
1 teaspoon French mustard
½ teaspoon castor sugar
salt and freshly ground pepper

Slice the peppers very thinly and place in a bowl with the
mushrooms, celery and onion. Pour the dressing ingredients into a
screw-top jar and shake well to mix. Pour over the vegetables and
stir until evenly coated. Cover and chill before serving.
    Serve with chicken, ham or cold bacon.
Serves 4-6

Marinated Mushrooms

1 ½ lb. (6 cups) small button
  mushrooms
½ pint (1 ¼ cups) white wine
½ teaspoon salt
2 teaspoons lemon juice
3 tablespoons olive oil
½ teaspoon paprika pepper

Garnish:
freshly chopped parsley
paprika pepper

Wash the mushrooms and dry on paper towels. Place in a pan with
the wine, salt and lemon juice. Simmer for 5 minutes. Strain off the
wine and allow the mushrooms to cool.
    Blend the oil and wine together and season with paprika pepper.
Pour over the mushrooms and garnish with chopped parsley and
paprika pepper.
    Serve chilled as an hors d'oeuvre or side salad.
Serves 4-6

Orange and Mushroom Medley

1 large orange
3 slices pineapple, diced
4 oz. (1 cup) button mushrooms,
  sliced
2 inch piece cucumber, diced

1 oz. (¼ cup) toasted almonds,
  flaked
1 oz. (2 T) rice, cooked
1 banana, sliced
2 teaspoons lemon juice

Carefully peel the skin and pith from the orange and cut into 1 inch pieces. Mix the pineapple with the orange. Add the mushrooms and cucumber to the fruit. Cover and keep in a cool place for 24 hours.

   Add the almonds, rice, banana and lemon juice and mix thoroughly. Chill the salad before serving.
Serves 4–6

Black Grape and Mushroom Salad

½ head chicory (Belgian endive)
small bunch spring onions
  (scallions)
2 hard-boiled eggs
small bunch black grapes, seeded
3 oz. (¾ cup) button mushrooms,
  sliced

Dressing:
¼ pint (⅔ cup) natural
  (unflavored) yogurt
freshly chopped mint

Arrange the chicory (Belgian endive) on a serving platter. Clean and trim the onions (scallions) and cut the eggs into quarters. Arrange the grapes, mushrooms, onions (scallions) and eggs in the centre of the dish.

   Mix together the yogurt and chopped mint and spoon over the salad or serve separately.
Serves 4

MARINATED MUSHROOMS (page 35),
ORANGE AND MUSHROOM MEDLEY,
BLACK GRAPE AND MUSHROOM SALAD
(Photograph: Mushroom Growers' Association)

Avocado and Corn Salad

1 avocado, peeled and chopped
1 × 15 oz. can asparagus, drained
  and chopped
1 × 11½ oz. can sweetcorn (kernel
  corn), drained

3 tablespoons tomato mayonnaise
salt and freshly ground pepper
paprika pepper

Place the avocado, asparagus and corn in a bowl. Mix in the tomato mayonnaise and season to taste with salt, pepper and paprika. Serve slightly chilled, sprinkled with a little paprika.
    This is a good accompaniment for barbecued meat.
Serves 4

Avocado Winter Salad

12 oz. (4½ cups) white cabbage,
  finely shredded
2 tablespoons grated onion
4 carrots, cut into sticks
2 oz. (½ cup) walnuts, chopped
4 tomatoes, roughly chopped

1 large ripe avocado
4 tablespoons (¼ cup) French
  dressing
salt and freshly ground pepper
parsley sprigs to garnish

Place the cabbage, onion, carrots, walnuts and tomatoes in a bowl and mix well. Peel and dice the avocado and toss in the dressing. Add to the salad and season with salt and pepper to taste. Turn onto a serving dish and garnish with parsley sprigs.
    Serve with hard-boiled eggs, cheese, cold meats or fish.
Serves 4-6
Ingredients such as chopped apple, celery, green pepper and sultanas (seedless white raisins) can also be added to the salad.

Tomato, Chicory (Belgian Endive) and Grape Salad

6 firm tomatoes, skinned
2 heads chicory (Belgian endive)
8 oz. (2 cups) black grapes
3 tablespoons French dressing

1 small onion, finely chopped
¼ teaspoon dried marjoram
salt and freshly ground pepper

Quarter the tomatoes and place in a bowl. Cut the chicory (Belgian endive) into pieces lengthways and add to the tomatoes. Halve the grapes and remove the seeds, then add to the salad.

Mix the French dressing with the onion, marjoram and salt and pepper to taste. Pour the dressing over the salad. Toss well and transfer to a serving bowl.
Serves 4

Tomato Coleslaw

12 oz. (4½ cups) white cabbage,
 finely shredded
8 oz. carrots, peeled and grated
2 oz. (⅓ cup) raisins
1 × 10 oz. can tomato soup

2 tablespoons wine vinegar
1 clove garlic, crushed
1 tablespoon freshly chopped
 parsley
salt and freshly ground pepper

Mix the cabbage, carrots and raisins together. Pour the soup into a separate bowl and add the vinegar, crushed garlic, parsley and salt and pepper to taste. Blend thoroughly and pour over the salad. Mix well and transfer to a serving bowl.
Serves 4

Crunchy Melon Salad

2 oz. (½ cup) walnuts, chopped
2 oz. (⅓ cup) raisins
1 tablespoon finely chopped onion
3 tablespoons French dressing
½ teaspoon French mustard
2 tablespoons double (heavy) cream

2 tablespoons freshly chopped
  parsley
½ Honeydew melon
1 head lettuce
parsley sprigs to garnish

Mix together the walnuts, raisins and onion. Blend the French dressing with the French mustard, cream and parsley. Peel the melon, remove the seeds and dice the flesh. Mix with the nut mixture and dressing. Cover and leave to stand for 30 minutes.

Arrange the lettuce on 4 individual dishes or 1 serving platter and spoon the melon salad into the centre. Garnish with parsley sprigs and serve with cold meats, salami, sardines or cottage cheese.
Serves 4

Crunchy Bean Salad

1 × 15 oz. can baked beans
4-5 spring onions (scallions),
  chopped
4 oz. (½ cup) French (green)
  beans, cooked and diced
1 small green pepper, seeded and
  chopped

Dressing:
2 tablespoons wine vinegar
1 tablespoon salad oil
salt and freshly ground pepper

Place the baked beans, spring onions (scallions), French (green) beans and pepper in a large bowl. Pour the oil and vinegar into a screw-top jar and add salt and pepper to taste. Shake the jar vigorously then pour the dressing over the bean mixture and stir well. Serve cold with cooked meats, hard-boiled eggs or cheese.
Serves 4

CRUNCHY MELON SALAD
(Photograph: Carmel Produce Information Bureau)

Broad (Lima) Bean Salad

1 × 10 oz. can broad (lima) beans
1 onion, sliced
4 tablespoons (¼ cup) salad oil

2 tablespoons wine vinegar
salt and freshly ground pepper
pinch of nutmeg

Drain the beans and place in a bowl with the onion. Pour the oil and vinegar into a screw-top jar and add salt, pepper and nutmeg to taste. Shake the jar vigorously then pour the dressing over the beans and onion. Mix well and chill before serving.
    This is an excellent accompaniment to cold ham or tongue.
Serves 4

Baked Bean and Celery Salad

1 × 15 oz. can baked beans
2 sticks celery, chopped
1 dessert apple, cored and diced

2 tablespoons mayonnaise
salt and freshly ground pepper
freshly chopped parsley to garnish

Place the baked beans in a serving dish with the celery and apple. Stir in the mayonnaise and season to taste with salt and pepper. Sprinkle with chopped parsley before serving.
Serves 4

Red Cabbage Salad

8 oz. (3 cups) red cabbage, finely
  shredded
2 dessert apples, cored and sliced
4 sticks celery, chopped

Dressing:
1 teaspoon salt
¼ teaspoon freshly ground pepper
1 tablespoon sugar
2 teaspoons French mustard
2 teaspoons onion powder
¼ pint (⅔ cup) vegetable oil
3 tablespoons cider vinegar

Mix together the cabbage, apples and celery. Blend the dressing
ingredients thoroughly and pour over the salad. Mix well, cover and
marinate in the refrigerator overnight.
   Serve with cold pork or sausages.
Serves 4–6

Italian Salad

4 oz. (1 cup) pasta shells
8 oz. (1½ cups) courgettes
  (zucchini), sliced
1 × 7 oz. can sweetcorn (kernel
  corn), drained

4 tablespoons (¼ cup) French
  dressing
salt and freshly ground pepper

Cook the pasta in boiling salted water until 'al dente' (just tender to
the bite), drain and rinse thoroughly. Cook the courgettes (zucchini)
in boiling salted water for 5 minutes and drain.
   Mix together the pasta, courgettes (zucchini), corn and French
dressing. Toss well to coat in the dressing and season to taste with
salt and pepper. Transfer to a serving bowl and serve with hot or
cold meats.
Serves 4

HOT SNACKS

Cheese and Mushroom Fondue

½ clove garlic
¼ pint (⅔ cup) dry (hard) cider
1 teaspoon lemon juice
14 oz. (3½ cups) Gouda cheese, grated
1 tablespoon cornflour (cornstarch)
1½ tablespoons gin, whisky, brandy or sherry

freshly ground pepper
pinch of grated nutmeg
4 oz. (1 cup) button mushrooms, chopped
French loaf, cut into cubes, to serve

Rub the inside of an earthenware pan with the cut garlic and place a little finely chopped garlic in the pan. Pour in the cider and lemon juice. Heat slowly until the cider is nearly boiling.

Gradually add the grated cheese, a little at a time, stirring continuously with a fork, until all the cheese has melted. When the mixture is boiling, blend the cornflour (cornstarch) with the gin (or alternative spirit) until smooth, and stir into the fondue. Add pepper and nutmeg to taste, and the chopped mushrooms and mix well.

Serve the fondue in the earthenware pan. The cubed bread is speared with a long fork and dipped into the fondue.
Serves 6–8

CHEESE AND MUSHROOM FONDUE,
ORANGE AND CUCUMBER SALAD *(page 34)*
(Photograph: Dutch Dairy Bureau)

Ham, Cheese and Apple Toast

3 dessert apples, cored
juice of ½ lemon
8 oz. (2 cups) Cheddar cheese,
  grated
4 teaspoons Worcestershire sauce

4 large thick slices bread
butter
4 slices cooked ham
watercress to garnish

Cut one unpeeled apple into 8 thin rings and dip in the lemon juice.
Grate the other two apples and mix with the grated cheese. Stir in
the Worcestershire sauce.

Toast the bread and spread with butter. Place a ham slice on each
piece of toast and top with the cheese mixture. Place under a
moderate grill (broiler) for 3–4 minutes until the cheese has melted
and is golden brown.

Garnish each slice of toast with 2 apple rings and a sprig of
watercress.
Serves 4

Grilled Cheese Medley

8 oz. (2 cups) onion, chopped
2 oz. (¼ cup) butter
1 tablespoon oil
8 oz. (12 slices) bacon, chopped
1 red pepper, seeded and cut into
  strips

1½ lb. potatoes, cooked
salt and freshly ground pepper
6 oz. (1½ cups) Gouda cheese,
  grated

Fry the onion in the butter and oil until transparent. Add the bacon
and red pepper and cook for 5–10 minutes. Slice the potatoes, add to
the pan and cook for a further 5 minutes, stirring continuously.
Season to taste with salt and pepper and sprinkle with the grated
cheese. Place under a hot grill (broiler) to brown.
Serves 4

Savoury Cheese Panperdy

4 oz. (½ cup) butter
6 slices bread, cubed
6 large eggs
1 tablespoon freshly chopped chives
1 tablespoon freshly chopped
  parsley

salt and freshly ground pepper
6 oz. (1½ cups) Gouda cheese,
  grated

Heat 2 oz. (¼ cup) of the butter and toss the bread in the pan until golden brown and crisp. Drain on paper towels. Keep hot.

Beat the eggs and add the herbs, salt and pepper. Melt the remaining butter in a large pan. Pour the egg mixture into the pan and cook over a moderate heat, moving occasionally with a spatula, until set.

Arrange the bread cubes and grated cheese over the omelette, cut into 4 pieces and serve immediately with salad and rolls.
Serves 4

Cheese Sizzlers

4 soft white (hamburger) rolls
4 oz. (½ cup) pâté or ham spread
1½ oz. (3 T) butter
8 oz. (2 cups) onion, chopped
pinch of dried thyme

4 tablespoons (¼ cup) tomato
  ketchup
8 oz. (2 cups) Gouda cheese,
  grated

Split the rolls in half and toast. Spread with the pâté or ham spread. Melt the butter and fry the onions until soft. Stir in the thyme and tomato ketchup and spread over the pâté or ham.

Top each roll half with grated cheese and place under a hot grill (broiler) until the cheese melts and is lightly browned.
Serves 4

Egg Pizzas

1 small onion, finely grated
3 tablespoons tomato purée (paste)
1 teaspoon oregano
salt and freshly ground pepper
4 flat bread rolls
8 hard-boiled eggs

8 black olives
8 oz. (2 cups) cheese, grated
2 eggs, beaten
½ teaspoon prepared mustard
watercress sprigs to garnish

Mix together the onion, tomato purée (paste), oregano, salt and pepper. Split the bread rolls and spread the mixture over each half.

Cut the hard-boiled eggs in half lengthways and place 2 halves on each half roll, cut side down. Halve the olives and remove the stones (pits) then arrange around the eggs.

Mix together the grated cheese, beaten eggs and mustard. Spread over the eggs and bake in a hot oven, 425°F, Gas Mark 7 for 10-15 minutes until the pizzas are risen and browned. Serve garnished with watercress.
Serves 4

Baked Potatoes with Cottage Cheese

4 large potatoes, scrubbed
8 oz. (1 cup) cottage cheese
2 tomatoes, skinned and chopped

1 tablespoon freshly chopped chives
2 tablespoons single (light) cream
salt and freshly ground pepper

Bake the potatoes in their skins in a moderately hot oven, 375°F, Gas Mark 5 for 1¼ hours or until cooked through. Leave to cool a little then cut a slice from the top of each potato.

Remove the potato from the skins and place in a bowl. Add the cottage cheese, tomatoes, chives and cream. Mix thoroughly and season to taste with salt and pepper.

Spoon the mixture back into the potato cases and replace the 'lids'. Serve immediately or warm in a moderate oven for a few minutes.
Serves 4
Alternative ingredients, such as chopped ham, chopped cooked bacon, sweetcorn (kernel corn) and chopped parsley, can be used in the filling if preferred.

EGG PIZZAS
(Photograph: British Egg Information Service)

Toasted Sandwiches

8 oz. (1 cup) cooked turkey or
  chicken, finely diced
2 tablespoons mayonnaise
1 stick celery, finely chopped
4 oz. (1 cup) cheese, grated

1 × 7 oz. can sweetcorn (kernel
  corn), drained
8 slices wholemeal (wholewheat)
  bread
butter or margarine

Mix together the turkey or chicken, mayonnaise, celery, cheese and
corn. Spread the mixture over 4 slices of bread and top with the
remaining slices. Spread both sides of the sandwiches with butter or
margarine and brown both sides under the grill (broiler).
Serves 4

Danish Blue Decker Sandwiches

12 thick slices bread
butter or margarine
lettuce, shredded

8 thin slices cooked ham
8 oz. Danish blue cheese, sliced
4 tomatoes, sliced

Toast the bread on both sides, remove the crusts, and spread with
butter or margarine. Use three slices of bread for each sandwich.
Arrange lettuce on one slice and cover with two pieces of ham folded
into three and placed across the corners. Top with the second slice of
toast and cover with cheese and tomato slices. Cover with the third
slice of toast.

   Repeat with remaining ingredients to make four sandwiches. Serve
cut into triangles.
Serves 4

Southern Sandwiches

5 eggs
2 small bananas
2 oz. (1 cup) fresh white
  breadcrumbs
oil for frying
lard for frying

4 large slices wholemeal
  (wholewheat) bread
butter or margarine
1 × 7 oz. can sweetcorn (kernel
  corn)
cucumber slices to garnish

Beat one of the eggs on a small plate. Peel and slice the bananas
thickly, toss in the egg and then coat with the breadcrumbs. Fry the
banana in a little oil until golden and keep hot.

Wipe the pan with kitchen paper, then melt some lard and fry the
remaining eggs, one at a time. Toast the bread and spread thickly
with butter or margarine. Heat the corn in the can liquid and then
drain.

Arrange the corn, banana and a fried egg on each piece of toast.
Serve hot, garnished with cucumber slices.
Serves 4

Barbecue Buns

4 oz. (½ cup) minced (ground)
  beef
½ small onion, chopped
2 oz. (⅓ cup) sweetcorn (kernel
  corn), drained
4 tablespoons (¼ cup) barbecue
  sauce

¼ teaspoon chilli powder
1 tablespoon water
4 frankfurter sausages
4 bap (hamburger) buns

Place the ground beef and onion in a pan and cook until the meat is
browned. Drain off the fat. Add the corn, barbecue sauce, chilli
powder and water. Mix well and simmer for about 15 minutes.

Heat the frankfurters in water but do not boil. Split the buns in
half and toast. Place a frankfurter in each and spoon the meat sauce
over. Serve immediately.
Serves 4

Frankfurter Fancy

butter
6 slices white bread
6 slices processed cheese
6 frankfurter sausages

6 large mushrooms
1 oz. (2T) margarine, melted
watercress to garnish

Spread butter over both sides of the bread. Place a slice of cheese on each bread slice and a frankfurter across the centre. Bend the bread and cheese around the sausage and secure each one with 2 cocktail sticks (toothpicks). Put a whole mushroom on each sandwich and arrange them in an ovenproof dish.

Brush the mushrooms with the melted margarine and bake in a hot oven, 425°F, Gas Mark 7 for 10 minutes. Serve hot, garnished with watercress.
Serves 6

Torpedo Burgers

½ oz. (1T) butter
1 onion, thinly sliced
1 tablespoon Worcestershire sauce
3 tablespoons tomato ketchup

salt and freshly ground pepper
4 pork (link) sausages
4 long white rolls
watercress to garnish

Melt the butter in a pan and fry the onion gently for 10 minutes. Stir in the Worcestershire sauce and tomato ketchup, reheat and season to taste with salt and pepper.

Grill (broil) the sausages until cooked. Warm the rolls and split open. Place a sausage on the bottom half of each roll and spoon the onion mixture over the top. Replace the top of the roll and serve immediately, garnished with watercress.
Serves 4

TUNA-STUFFED AUBERGINE (EGGPLANT) (page 60)
(Photograph: Carmel Produce Information Bureau)

Stuffed Sausage Loaf

2 'Vienna' loaves
6 oz. (¾ cup) unsalted (sweet)
  butter
2 lb. (link) sausages
2 green peppers, seeded and
  chopped
4 sticks celery, chopped

4 oz. (1 cup) button mushrooms,
  sliced
12 oz. (3 cups) Gouda cheese,
  grated
2 eggs, beaten
salt and freshly ground pepper

Slice the loaves lengthways leaving a hinge down one side. Scoop
out the soft bread from the centres. Melt 3 oz. (6T) of the butter and
use to brush the inside of the bread shells. Place the soft bread on a
baking sheet and bake in a moderately hot oven, 375°F, Gas Mark 5
until crisp.

Cook the sausages in the oven and cut into ½ inch slices. Fry the
chopped pepper, celery and mushrooms in the remaining butter until
soft, then mix with the sausages.

Place the bread from the oven in a plastic bag and roll with a
rolling pin to make fine crumbs. Add to the sausage mixture with
the grated cheese, beaten eggs, salt and pepper. Pile the mixture into
the bread shells and partially close the lid. Wrap the loaves in
aluminium foil and bake in a moderately hot oven, 375°F, Gas Mark
5 for 25–30 minutes until the bread is crisp. Serve hot with a selection
of salads.

Serves 6–8
The loaves can also be served cold which makes them ideal for
picnics.

Hamburgers

2 soft white (hamburger) rolls, cut
  in half and toasted
Hamburger:
1 lb. (2 cups) minced (ground) beef
salt and freshly ground pepper
1 tablespoon chopped onion
1 tablespoon tomato ketchup
oil for frying

Relish:
1 × 11½ oz. can sweetcorn (kernel
  corn), drained
¼ cucumber, peeled and chopped
4 small gherkins (1 dill pickle),
  chopped
3 teaspoons Worcestershire sauce

To make the hamburgers, mix the beef with salt and pepper, onion
and tomato ketchup. Divide the mixture into 4. Lightly grease the
inside of a large plain pastry cutter and spoon one portion into the
centre. Press to flatten and remove the cutter. Make 3 more burgers
in the same way.

   Heat some oil in a frying pan (skillet) and fry 2 burgers at a time
over a high heat for 1 minute each side. Reduce the heat and cook for
a further 5 minutes each side. Drain well and place on a toasted roll
half. Mix together the corn, cucumber, gherkins (dill pickle) and
Worcestershire sauce. Spoon over the hamburgers and serve.
Serves 4

Fish Finger Open Sandwiches

8 fish fingers
4 slices bread
butter or margarine
1 hard-boiled egg, sliced
2 slices pineapple, halved

1 tomato, sliced
2 rashers (slices) bacon, grilled
  (broiled) and cut in half
watercress to garnish

Cook the fish fingers under a medium hot grill (broiler) and allow to
cool a little. Toast the bread and spread with butter or margarine.
Arrange the fish fingers, egg slices, pineapple, tomato, and bacon on
the slices of toast. Serve garnished with watercress.
Serves 4

Corn-on-the-cob

4 plump corn cobs
2 oz. (¼ cup) butter
salt and freshly ground pepper

Remove the outside leaves and silky threads from the cobs and place
in boiling water. (Do not add salt as this toughens the corn.) Cook
for 12–20 minutes depending on size. Drain well and place on a plate
or special corn serving dish.

Serve with butter and a generous amount of salt and freshly
ground pepper.
Serves 4

Quick Corn Risotto

4 oz. (½ cup) long-grain rice
2 oz. (¼ cup) butter
1 onion, peeled and chopped
4 oz. (1 cup) mushrooms, sliced
2 rashers (slices) bacon, chopped
8 oz. (1 cup) cooked meat, diced

1 × 11½ oz. can sweetcorn (kernel
 corn), drained
salt and freshly ground pepper
2 oz. (½ cup) Parmesan cheese,
 grated
2 tomatoes, sliced, to garnish

Cook the rice in boiling salted water for about 12 minutes until
cooked. Drain well.

Melt the butter in a pan and fry the onion until soft. Add the
mushrooms and bacon and continue frying for 2–3 minutes. Stir in
the cooked meat, corn, and salt and pepper to taste. Add the rice and
heat gently until really hot.

Pile onto a hot serving dish, sprinkle with the cheese and garnish
with tomato slices.
Serves 4

Piazza Pasta

8 oz. (2 cups) pasta shells
1 medium onion, chopped
1 clove garlic, crushed
2 oz. (¼ cup) butter
1 × 7 oz. can tuna
1 teaspoon grated lemon rind
2 tablespoons freshly chopped
  parsley

1 × 7 oz. can sweetcorn (kernel
  corn), drained
salt and freshly ground pepper
1 hard-boiled egg, quartered,
  to garnish

Cook the pasta in boiling salted water until 'al dente' (just tender to the bite), drain, rinse and keep hot.

Meanwhile, fry the onion and garlic in the butter. Drain the oil from the tuna and add the oil to the pan with the grated lemon rind and parsley. Stir well and add the flaked tuna and corn. Season to taste with salt and pepper and heat gently.

Fold in the hot pasta and spoon onto a warm serving dish. Serve garnished with hard-boiled egg.
Serves 4

Quick Bavarian Pizza

Scone (biscuit) dough:
4 oz. (1 cup) self-raising
  (self-rising) flour
½ teaspoon baking powder
½ teaspoon dry mustard
½ teaspoon salt
1 oz. (2 T) margarine
1 medium onion, grated
3 oz. (¾ cup) cheese, grated
½ teaspoon mixed dried herbs

1 egg
1 tablespoon milk
Topping:
¼ teaspoon dried oregano
4 tomatoes, skinned and sliced
2 oz. (½ cup) cheese, grated
4 oz. (1 cup) mushrooms, sliced
2 oz. smoked German sausage, cut
  into thin strips
parsley sprigs to garnish

Sift the flour, baking powder, dry mustard and salt into a mixing bowl. Add the margarine, onion, cheese, dried herbs, egg and milk. Mix with a wooden spoon to give a soft dough. Turn onto a floured surface and knead until smooth. Roll out to a flat round 9 inches in diameter and place on a greased baking sheet.

Sprinkle the oregano over the dough and cover with a layer of tomatoes, cheese, mushrooms and German sausage.

Bake in moderately hot oven, 400°F, Gas Mark 6 for 20-25 minutes.

Garnish with parsley and serve hot or cold with a green salad.
Serves 4

Bacon and Tomato Pizza

Scone (biscuit) dough:
8 oz. (2 cups) self-raising
  (self-rising) flour
¼ teaspoon salt
2 oz. (¼ cup) margarine
¼ pint (⅔ cup) milk

Topping:
1 oz. (2 T) butter
2 onions, thinly sliced
1 tablespoon Worcestershire sauce
6 tomatoes, skinned and sliced
salt and freshly ground pepper
6 oz. (9 slices) streaky (fatty)
  bacon, rind removed

Sift the flour and salt into a bowl and rub in the margarine until the mixture resembles fine breadcrumbs. Add the milk and mix to a soft dough. Knead on a floured surface until smooth and roll out to a rectangle 10 × 7 inches. Place on a greased baking sheet.

For the topping, melt the butter in a pan and fry the onions gently for 10 minutes. Stir in the Worcestershire sauce and spread the mixture over the scone (biscuit) dough. Arrange the sliced tomatoes on top and sprinkle with salt and pepper. Bake in a hot oven, 425°F, Gas Mark 7 for 20 minutes.

Stretch the bacon on a board with the back of a knife. Cut each rasher (slice) in half lengthwise and arrange the strips in a diagonal lattice pattern over the tomatoes. Return to the oven and bake for a further 8–10 minutes until the bacon is cooked. Serve cut into slices with salad.
Serves 4-6

Potato and Aubergine (Eggplant) Bake

2 lb. potatoes, peeled
2 large aubergines (eggplant)
2 onions, sliced
1 tablespoon oil

8 oz. (2 cups) Cheddar cheese,
  grated
salt and freshly ground pepper

Parboil the potatoes in boiling salted water for 10 minutes, drain and slice. Slice the aubergines (eggplant) and arrange a few slices in the bottom of a buttered ovenproof dish. Fry the onions in the oil until just soft. Arrange the vegetables in layers, sprinkling each one with grated cheese, salt and pepper.

Cover the dish and bake in a moderately hot oven, 375°F, Gas Mark 5 for 1½ hours or until golden brown.
Serves 4-6

Tuna-stuffed Aubergine (Eggplant)

2 large aubergines (eggplant)
2 tablespoons oil
1 onion, chopped
1 × 15 oz. can tomatoes, drained
2 tablespoons tomato purée (paste)
1 clove garlic, crushed

1 teaspoon mixed dried herbs
salt and freshly ground pepper
1 × 8 oz. can tuna, drained
4 oz. (1 cup) Cheddar cheese,
  grated

Cut the aubergines (eggplant) in half lengthways. Using a grapefruit knife, carefully remove the inside flesh and chop roughly.

Heat the oil in a pan and fry the onion until brown. Add the tomatoes, tomato purée (paste), garlic, aubergine (eggplant) flesh, herbs and salt and pepper. Bring to the boil, then simmer for 15-20 minutes. Flake the tuna and stir into the mixture.

Pile into the aubergine (eggplant) shells and sprinkle with grated cheese. Cover and bake in a moderately hot oven, 375°F, Gas Mark 5 for 30-35 minutes until golden brown.
Serves 4

POTATO AND AUBERGINE (EGGPLANT) BAKE
(Photograph: Carmel Produce Information Bureau)

Stuffed Peppers

4 green peppers
2 oz. (4 T) long-grain rice, cooked
4 tomatoes, skinned and chopped
3 tablespoons tomato purée (paste)
1 onion, finely chopped
12 oz. (1½ cups) cooked cod, flaked

salt
1 teaspoon dried thyme
2 oz. (½ cup) cheese, grated
chicken stock
freshly chopped parsley to garnish

Cut the peppers in half across the stalks, remove the seeds and wash well. Blanch the pepper cases in boiling salted water for 3 minutes.

Mix the rice with the tomatoes, tomato purée (paste), onion, fish, salt to taste and the thyme. Pile the mixture into the pepper cases and sprinkle with the grated cheese.

Place in a shallow ovenproof dish and pour a little stock around the peppers to keep them moist during cooking. Bake in a moderately hot oven, 375°F, Gas Mark 5 for 25 minutes. Serve hot, garnished with parsley.
Serves 4

Savoury Vol-au-vents

8 vol-au-vent cases
12 oz. smoked whiting fillets
½ pint (1¼ cups) tomato juice
2 tablespoons water
salt and freshly ground pepper

12 oz. (3 cups) small button mushrooms
2 oz. (¼ cup) butter
2 teaspoons cornflour (cornstarch)

Bake the vol-au-vent cases in a hot oven, 425°F, Gas Mark 7 until well risen and golden. Remove the tops and lift out any soft pastry from the centre. Return the cases to the oven to crisp.

Place the fish fillets in a shallow pan with the tomato juice and water. Sprinkle with salt and pepper, cover the pan and simmer for 7-10 minutes until the fish flakes easily.

Keep 4 mushrooms whole and slice the remainder. In another pan heat the butter and cook all the mushrooms. Lift out the whole mushrooms and keep them warm. Flake the fish and add the mushrooms with the tomato juice. Blend the cornflour (cornstarch) with a little water and add to the pan. Cook gently until the mixture thickens. Adjust the seasoning and use the mixture to fill the vol-au-vent cases. Top each with half a mushroom and serve hot.
Serves 4

Crispy Salmon Balls with Spicy Dip

1 × 6 serving packet instant potato
3/4 pint (2 cups) boiling water
1 egg, beaten
1 × 7½ oz. can pink salmon,
 flaked
1 small onion, grated
1 tablespoon Worcestershire sauce
salt and freshly ground pepper
fat or oil for deep frying

Coating:
1 egg, beaten
golden crumbs

Sauce:
6 tablespoons thick mayonnaise
2 tablespoons tomato purée (paste)
2 teaspoons Worcestershire sauce
1 tablespoon freshly chopped
 parsley
1 small onion, grated
salt and freshly ground pepper

Reconstitute the potato with the boiling water. Stir in the beaten egg, flaked salmon, onion and Worcestershire sauce. Beat well and season to taste with salt and pepper. Cool and chill before shaping the mixture into 20 balls, approximately 1¼ inches in diameter.

Dip each ball into the beaten egg and coat in the golden crumbs. Fry the balls in hot fat or oil for 3-4 minutes until crisp. Drain on paper towels.

To make the sauce, mix all the ingredients together with salt and pepper to taste. Serve with the salmon balls.

Serves 4

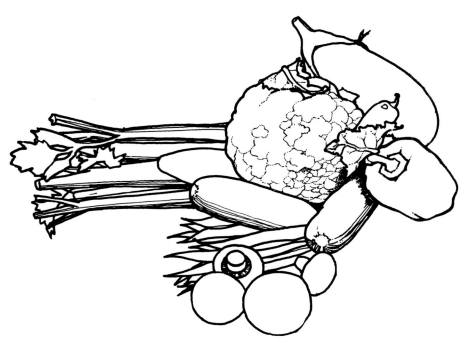

Avocado Grill (Broil)

4 oz. (6 slices) bacon
4 soft bread rolls
butter

1 avocado, stone (pit) removed
prepared mustard
6 oz. (1½ cups) cheese, grated

Cut the bacon into strips and fry until crisp. Keep hot. Split the bread rolls, toast on one side and spread with butter.

Peel and thinly slice the avocado, reserving some for garnishing. Arrange on the rolls and brush lightly with mustard. Sprinkle the grated cheese over the top making sure the avocado is well covered.

Grill (broil) until the cheese has melted. Top with the bacon strips and remaining pieces of avocado. Serve immediately.
Serves 4

Speedy Beef and Rice

1 × 10½ oz. can condensed onion
  soup
¼ pint (⅔ cup) water
1 × 15 oz. can minced (ground)
  beef and gravy

3 oz. (½ cup) long-grain rice
2 tablespoons Worcestershire sauce
salt and freshly ground pepper
8 oz. (1½ cups) peas, cooked
1 tomato, sliced, to garnish

Place all the ingredients, except the peas and tomato, in a pan. Bring to the boil, stirring, and simmer without a lid for 20–25 minutes until the rice is cooked.

Turn into a serving dish and arrange the peas around the edge. Garnish with tomato slices.
Serves 4

AVOCADO GRILL (BROIL)
(Photograph: Carmel Produce Information Bureau)

Quick Vegetable Casserole

8 oz. (2 cups) leeks, sliced
3 tomatoes, skinned
8 oz. (1⅓ cups) cooked potatoes,
  diced
1 × 10 oz. can condensed chicken
  soup

½ teaspoon mixed dried herbs
salt and freshly ground pepper
4 oz. (1 cup) Gouda cheese, grated

Wash the leeks and cook in boiling salted water for 10 minutes.
Drain well. Cut the tomatoes into wedges and mix with the leeks,
potatoes, chicken soup, herbs and salt and pepper to taste.

Place in an ovenproof dish, sprinkle with the grated cheese and
bake in a moderately hot oven, 375°F, Gas Mark 5 for 15-20 minutes.
Serves 4

Dutch Cheese Soufflé

2 oz. (¼ cup) butter
2 oz. (½ cup) plain (all-purpose)
  flour
½ pint (1¼ cups) milk
¼ teaspoon cayenne pepper

pinch of dry mustard
salt
3 large eggs, separated
4 oz. (1 cup) Edam cheese, grated
freshly chopped parsley to garnish

Place the butter, flour, milk, cayenne pepper, mustard and salt in a
saucepan and whisk over a gentle heat until thick. Cool slightly, then
beat in the egg yolks, one at a time. Fold in the grated cheese. Whisk
the egg whites until stiff and fold into the cheese mixture with a
metal spoon.

Pour into a 7 inch buttered soufflé dish and bake in a preheated
moderately hot oven, 375°F, Gas Mark 5 for 40-45 minutes. Serve
immediately, garnished with chopped parsley.
Serves 4

Peanut Soup

3 tablespoons smooth peanut butter
2 oz. (⅓ cup) soft (light) brown
 sugar
½ pint (1¼ cups) milk
1 oz. (2T) butter
1 onion, chopped
¾ pint (2 cups) chicken stock

1 × 7 oz. can sweetcorn (kernel
 corn), drained
5 oz. (¾ cup) salted peanuts
salt and freshly ground pepper
8 oz. (2 cups) Gouda cheese,
 grated

Place the peanut butter, sugar and milk in a saucepan and heat gently, stirring until smooth.

In another pan, melt the butter and sauté the onion until soft. Add the peanut sauce and chicken stock and heat until the sauce comes to the boil. Reduce the heat and add the corn and peanuts. Season to taste with salt and pepper and heat gently for 5 minutes.

Add the cheese and stir until melted. Serve hot with crusty rolls.
Serves 6

Cheese and Celery Soup

1 oz. (2T) butter
1 large onion, chopped
2 sticks celery, chopped
½ pint (1¼ cups) water
1 pint (2½ cups) milk

1 tablespoon cornflour (cornstarch)
2 tablespoons Worcestershire sauce
7 oz. (1¾ cups) Cheddar cheese,
 grated
salt and freshly ground pepper

Melt the butter in a large pan and fry the onion and celery gently for 5 minutes. Add the water and milk and bring to the boil. Simmer for 20 minutes.

Blend the cornflour (cornstarch) with the Worcestershire sauce, stir into the soup and bring to the boil, stirring. Remove from the heat and stir in 6 oz. (1½ cups) of the cheese. Season to taste with salt and pepper and reheat without boiling. Serve garnished with the remaining cheese.
Serves 4

DRESSINGS

The following dressings can be served with green or mixed salads.
  The French dressing recipe can be used with any salad recipe in this book which does not give the ingredients for a dressing.

French Dressing (Sauce Vinaigrette)

¼ teaspoon dry mustard
¼ teaspoon salt
⅛ teaspoon freshly ground pepper

¼ teaspoon sugar
1 tablespoon wine vinegar
2 tablespoons olive oil

Put the mustard, salt, pepper and sugar in a bowl, add the vinegar and stir until well blended. Beat in the oil and use at once. If left to stand the oil will separate so the dressing should be shaken or whisked before serving. (These are basic proportions which can be increased for larger quantities.)

Variations
One or more of the following ingredients can be added to the above dressing:

1 clove garlic, crushed
½ teaspoon curry powder
2 teaspoons freshly chopped parsley
2 teaspoons freshly chopped chives
1-2 teaspoons Worcestershire sauce

pinch of dried thyme
1 tablespoon finely chopped olives
1 oz. (¼ cup) blue cheese,
  crumbled

ITALIAN CHICKEN WITH TUNA SAUCE *(page 14)*
(Photograph: Buxted Advisory Service)

Basic Yogurt Dressing

¼ pint (⅔ cup) natural
 (unflavored) yogurt
2 tablespoons single (light) cream
3 teaspoons lemon juice

1 teaspoon icing (confectioners')
 sugar
salt and freshly ground pepper

Put the yogurt into a bowl and beat in the cream, lemon juice and
sugar. Season to taste with salt and pepper. Leave in a cool place for
15-20 minutes before serving.

Variations
One or more of the following ingredients can be added to the above
dressing:

3 tablespoons finely chopped
 watercress
2 teaspoons curry powder

1 teaspoon Worcestershire sauce
1 tablespoon tomato sauce

Blue Cheese Dressing

4 oz. (1 cup) blue cheese, crumbled
4 oz. (½ cup) cream cheese
½ clove garlic, finely chopped

¼ pint (⅔ cup) milk
salt and freshly ground pepper

Mash the blue cheese and cream cheese together and stir in the garlic.
Gradually beat in the milk and season to taste with salt and pepper.
Chill in the refrigerator and serve with green or mixed salads.

Classic Mayonnaise

1 egg yolk
½ teaspoon dry mustard
½ teaspoon salt
¼ teaspoon freshly ground pepper

½ teaspoon sugar
¼ pint (⅔ cup) salad oil
1 tablespoon white wine vinegar or
  lemon juice

Place the egg yolk in a bowl with the seasoning and sugar. Mix
thoroughly, then add the oil, a drop at a time, stirring briskly with a
wooden spoon. The sauce should become thick and smooth. Add the
vinegar or lemon juice gradually and mix thoroughly.

A whisk can be used instead of a wooden spoon. Alternatively an
electric blender makes the process easier and quicker.

Variations
One or more of the following ingredients can be added to the basic
mayonnaise:

2 teaspoons chopped capers
4 tablespoons (¼ cup) whipped
  cream
1 tablespoon horseradish sauce
2 tablespoons freshly chopped herbs

2 tablespoons finely chopped
  cucumber
2 spring onions (scallions), chopped
1 oz. (¼ cup) blue cheese,
  crumbled

Soured Cream Dressing

¼ pint (⅔ cup) soured cream
1 tablespoon milk
1 tablespoon lemon juice

1 teaspoon icing (confectioners')
  sugar
salt and freshly ground pepper

Combine the soured cream, milk and lemon juice. Stir in the sugar
and season to taste with salt and pepper. Leave in a cool place for 15
minutes before serving.

If a thinner dressing is preferred a little extra milk can be added.

Variations
One or more of the following ingredients can be added to the above
dressing:

2 oz. (½ cup) walnuts, chopped
¼ cucumber, peeled and grated
2 teaspoons tomato purée (paste)

1 teaspoon prepared mustard
1 tablespoon freshly chopped chives
2 teaspoons grated horseradish

SANDWICHES

Egg and Salami Rolls

4 long or round rolls
2 oz. (¼ cup) butter, softened
4 lettuce leaves

2 hard-boiled eggs, chopped
2-3 tablespoons mayonnaise
2 oz. (¼ cup) salami, sliced

Split the rolls into 3 without cutting through completely. Arrange
lettuce leaves on both layers. Divide the egg between the top layers
of the rolls and spread with mayonnaise. Place salami slices on the
bottom layers and serve.
Makes 4

Slimline Squares

2 thin slices white bread
1 teaspoon yeast extract
4 oz. (½ cup) cottage cheese

1 tablespoon freshly chopped
  watercress
salt and freshly ground pepper

Spread both slices of the bread thinly with yeast extract. Mix the
cottage cheese with the watercress and salt and pepper to taste.
Spread over the yeast extract and sandwich the bread together. Cut
into 4 squares.
Serves 1

EGG AND SALAMI ROLL,
SLIMLINE SQUARES, STRIPED TRIANGLES *(page 74)*
(Photograph: Flour Advisory Bureau)

Striped Triangles

4 oz. (½ cup) cooked ham, finely
  chopped
2 oz. (¼ cup) butter, softened
2 teaspoons Worcestershire sauce
¼ teaspoon prepared mustard

salt and freshly ground pepper
16 slices white bread
6 oz. (¾ cup) pâté
8 slices brown bread

Cream the ham with the butter and add the Worcestershire sauce, mustard and salt and pepper to taste. Spread 8 slices of white bread with the filling. Spread the remaining 8 slices of white bread with the pâté and place on top of the ham filling.

Top with the brown bread to make double decker sandwiches. Cut each round into 4 triangles.
Makes 8 rounds

Hawaiian Layer Sandwich

8 slices bread
butter, softened
lettuce leaves
4 slices cooked ham

8 oz. (1 cup) cottage cheese with
  pineapple
salt and freshly ground pepper
parsley sprigs to garnish

Spread the bread with butter. Cover 4 slices with lettuce and a slice of ham. Spread with the cottage cheese and season well with salt and pepper. Cover with the remaining slices of bread.

Cut into triangles and serve garnished with parsley sprigs.
Makes 4 rounds

Bacon and Corn Sandwiches

3 oz. (⅓ cup) cream cheese
3 rashers (slices) bacon, crisply
  fried and crumbled
1 × 7 oz. can sweetcorn (kernel
  corn), drained
1 oz. (¼ cup) button mushrooms,
  finely chopped

salt and freshly ground pepper
8 thin slices wholemeal
  (wholewheat) bread
butter, softened
mayonnaise
2 tablespoons freshly chopped
  parsley

Mix together the cream cheese, bacon, corn and mushrooms. Season to taste with salt and pepper.

Cut the crusts from the bread and spread each slice with butter. Cover 4 slices of bread with the bacon mixture and top with the remaining bread slices. Cut each sandwich in half. Spread the tops with mayonnaise and sprinkle with parsley.
Makes 4 rounds

Decker Sandwiches

2 fillings
8 slices brown bread, buttered
4 slices white bread, buttered

Spread 4 slices of brown bread with one filling, cover with 4 slices of white bread then spread these with the second filling. Cover with the remaining slices of brown bread. Press down well. Remove the crusts and cut each sandwich into triangles, squares or fingers.

Use 2 of the following for the fillings:

Cream Cheese and Chive
4 oz. (½ cup) cream cheese
2 tablespoons milk

1 tablespoon freshly chopped chives

Beat the ingredients together until smooth and creamy.

Devilled Ham and Grated Carrot
4 oz. (½ cup) cooked ham, finely chopped
1 medium carrot, grated
1 teaspoon Worcestershire sauce

¼ teaspoon prepared mustard
2 oz. (¼ cup) butter, softened
salt and freshly ground pepper

Blend all the ingredients together thoroughly and season to taste with salt and pepper.

Egg and Tomato
4 hard-boiled eggs, chopped
2 oz. (¼ cup) butter, softened

4 tablespoons (¼ cup) tomato ketchup
salt and freshly ground pepper

Cream all the ingredients together and season to taste with salt and pepper.

COLD SNACKS

Dips are quick and easy to make and can be used in many ways.

Serve with a selection of raw vegetables, crisps (potato chips) and savoury biscuits (crackers) when entertaining. Spread a little on biscuits (crackers) for a quick snack or use the mixture as a filling for rolls, sandwiches and vol-au-vents.

Avocado Dip

2 teaspoons (1½ teaspoons)
  gelatine
1 teaspoon sugar
3 tablespoons water
¼ pint (⅔ cup) double (heavy)
  cream, whipped
4 tablespoons (¼ cup) mayonnaise

1 medium avocado, peeled and
  mashed
¼ pint (⅔ cup) cold water
1 teaspoon salt
1 teaspoon finely chopped onion

Sprinkle the gelatine and sugar over the water in a heatproof bowl, then place in a pan of gently simmering water and stir until dissolved.

Mix the cream with the mayonnaise then add the gelatine mixture, stirring continuously. Blend in the avocado pulp, cold water, salt and onion. Place in a bowl and chill before serving.
Serves 4–6

PEACH AND COTTAGE CHEESE SALAD *(page 19)*
(Photograph: Hellmans)

Egg and Avocado Dip

2 avocados
2 tomatoes, skinned and seeded
3 hard-boiled eggs, chopped
3 tablespoons lemon juice
2 tablespoons mayonnaise

Garnish:
paprika pepper
freshly chopped parsley

Cut the avocados in half, remove the stones (pits), carefully remove the flesh and dice. Roughly chop the tomatoes. Mix all the ingredients, except the garnish, and place in a blender for 20 seconds.

Spoon the cream dip into the avocado shells and serve sprinkled with paprika pepper and parsley.
Serves 8–10

Cheese and Gherkin (Dill Pickle) Dip

1 tablespoon (2¼ teaspoons)
 gelatine
¼ pint (⅔ cup) hot water
8 oz. (1 cup) cream cheese
1 tablespoon mayonnaise

1 small can evaporated milk
pinch of cayenne pepper
salt and freshly ground pepper
6 gherkins (small dill pickles),
 finely chopped, to garnish

Dissolve the gelatine in the hot water. Allow to cool.

Beat together the cream cheese and mayonnaise. Add the evaporated milk and gelatine solution, then whisk until thick. Season to taste with cayenne pepper, salt and pepper and fold in the chopped gherkins (dill pickles).

Transfer to a serving bowl and chill. If liked, garnish with gherkins (small dill pickles).
Serves 8–10

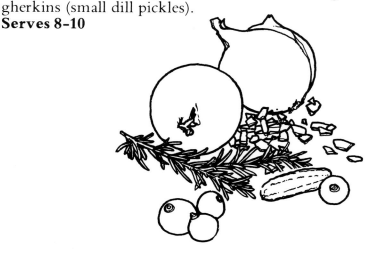

Salmon Dip

1 tablespoon (2 ¼ teaspoons)
  gelatine
¼ pint (⅔ cup) hot water
2 oz. (¼ cup) butter
1 hard-boiled egg yolk, sieved
  (strained)
salt

½ teaspoon prepared mustard
2 teaspoons vinegar
pinch of cayenne pepper
1 × 3 ½ oz. can red salmon, flaked
¼ pint (⅔ cup) milk
lemon slices to garnish

Dissolve the gelatine in the hot water. Allow to cool.

Cream together the butter and egg yolk, then add salt to taste, the mustard, vinegar and cayenne pepper. Mix in the cooled gelatine mixture, a little at a time, beating and whisking thoroughly with each addition. Stir in the flaked salmon and milk.

Pour into serving bowls and leave to become firm. Serve chilled, garnished with lemon slices.
Serves 6

Ham and Mushroom Dip

1 tablespoon (2 ¼ teaspoons)
  gelatine
¼ pint (⅔ cup) hot water
1 × 10 oz. can condensed cream of
  mushroom soup

pinch of cayenne pepper
2 oz. (¼ cup) ham, chopped
2 tablespoons double (heavy) cream
few raw mushrooms, sliced, to
  garnish

Dissolve the gelatine in the hot water. Stir in the mushroom soup. Add cayenne pepper to taste, the chopped ham and cream. Mix well and transfer to a serving bowl.

Chill before serving and garnish with mushroom slices.
Serves 6

Pork and Sausage Plait (Braid)

12 oz. (3 cups) puff pastry
8 oz. (1 cup) belly (fatty) pork,
  finely chopped
8 oz. (1 cup) pork sausagemeat

1 teaspoon dried basil
salt and freshly ground pepper
1 egg, beaten
watercress sprigs to garnish

Roll the pastry to a rectangle about 11 × 8 inches.

Mix the pork with the sausagemeat, basil, salt, pepper and half the beaten egg. Shape the pork mixture into a 4 inch roll and place down the centre of the pastry leaving equal borders. Cut ½ inch diagonal strips down each border, then fold them over the filling to give a plaited (braided) effect.

Brush with the remaining beaten egg and bake in a preheated hot oven, 425°F, Gas Mark 7 for 25–30 minutes. Leave to cool, then place on an oval serving dish. Garnish with watercress and serve cut into slices.
Serves 4

Corn Delight

8 oz. (1 cup) cream cheese
¼ pint (⅔ cup) soured cream
1 medium onion, finely chopped
2 tablespoons freshly chopped
  chives
1 red pepper, seeded and finely
  chopped

4 oz. (¾ cup) olives, stoned
  (pitted) and quartered
1 tablespoon lemon juice
1 × 11½ oz. can sweetcorn (kernel
  corn), drained

Beat the cream cheese and soured cream together until smooth. Stir in the onion, chives, red pepper, olives, lemon juice and corn. Mix well.

Transfer to a serving bowl and chill in the refrigerator. Serve with savoury biscuits (crackers) and raw vegetables.
Serves 12

PORK AND SAUSAGE PLAIT (BRAID)
(Photograph: British Meat Promotion Executive)

Cheesy Peaches

8 peach halves
8 oz. (1 cup) cottage cheese
3 sticks celery, chopped
4 walnuts, chopped
juice of 1/2 lemon

2 tablespoons cucumber spread
salt and freshly ground pepper
garlic salt
lettuce leaves

If using canned peaches drain off the juice. Mix together the cottage cheese, celery, walnuts, lemon juice and cucumber spread. Season to taste with salt, pepper and garlic salt. Pile the mixture into the peach halves.

Arrange lettuce leaves on 1 large or 4 individual plates and place the peaches on top.
Serves 4

Cheese Whirl Savoury

6 oz. (1 1/2 cups) Cheddar cheese, grated
2 tomatoes, skinned and mashed
1/4 pint (2/3 cup) double (heavy) cream
1 teaspoon mixed dried herbs
salt and freshly ground pepper

4 thick slices bread
butter
4 slices of salami
Garnish:
cucumber slices
watercress sprigs

Place the grated cheese in a bowl with the tomatoes, cream, mixed herbs and salt and pepper to taste. Mix well and place in a piping (pastry) bag fitted with a large star (fluted) nozzle.

Using a 3 inch cutter, press out a circle in each slice of bread. Lightly butter the rounds and place a piece of salami on top.

Pipe whirls of cheese mixture over the top and garnish with cucumber slices and watercress sprigs.
Serves 4

Cheese Balls

8 oz. (1 cup) cream cheese
2 oz. (¼ cup) butter
8 oz. (2 cups) button mushrooms,
sliced

1 × 7 oz. can sweetcorn (kernel
corn), drained
3 oz. (⅓ cup) smoked cream cheese
freshly chopped parsley to garnish

Beat together the cream cheese and butter until light and fluffy. Fold in the mushrooms and corn. Shape the mixture into a ball in a small bowl, cover and chill until firm.

Beat the smoked cheese until light and fluffy, cover and keep at room temperature. Place the cheese ball on a serving platter and cover the top with the smoked cheese. Chill in the refrigerator. Sprinkle with parsley and serve with cheese biscuits (crackers).
Serves 6

Slimmer's Savoury Grapefruit

4 grapefruit
8 oz. (2 cups) cucumber, chopped
4 oz. (1 cup) mushrooms, sliced
4 oz. (1 cup) Edam cheese, cubed
1 × 7 oz. can tuna, drained and
flaked

2 tomatoes, skinned, seeded and
chopped
2 teaspoons oil

Cut the grapefruit in a zig-zag design one-third of the way down. Remove the top and scrape out the flesh, reserving ¼ pint (⅔ cup) of the juice.

Mix together the cucumber, mushrooms, cheese, tuna, tomatoes and grapefruit flesh. Pile the mixture into the grapefruit shells. Mix the oil with the grapefruit juice and pour over the filling. Serve immediately.
Serves 4

Edam and Ham Rolls

8 oz. (2 cups) wholemeal
  (wholewheat) flour
1½ tablespoons baking powder
1 teaspoon salt
2 oz. (¼ cup) butter
¼ pint (⅔ cup) milk
8 slices cooked ham

4 teaspoons French mustard
8 oz. Edam cheese, cut into 3 inch
  sticks
8 bread rolls
beaten egg
1 oz. (¼ cup) Edam cheese, grated

Sift the flour into a bowl with the baking powder and salt. Rub in the butter until the mixture resembles fine breadcrumbs. Add the milk and mix to a firm dough. Turn onto a floured board and knead lightly. Keep cool.

Place the ham on a flat surface and spread with mustard. Divide the cheese sticks between the slices. Roll the ham around the cheese and place inside the bread rolls.

Divide the pastry dough into 8 and roll each piece to a 4 inch square. Place a ham roll in the centre of each square. With a sharp knife cut diagonal slits in the pastry down each side of the ham roll. Dampen the edges and fold in the dough at the top and bottom, then plait (braid) the strips over.

Place the rolls on a baking sheet and brush with beaten egg. Bake in a preheated moderately hot oven, 400°F, Gas Mark 6 for 20-25 minutes. Sprinkle with the grated cheese 5 minutes before the end of cooking time. Cool on a wire rack.
Serves 4-8

Ham Pinwheels

6 oz. (¾ cup) cream cheese
1 × 7 oz. can sweetcorn (kernel
  corn), drained

9 square slices cooked ham
1 × 15 oz. can asparagus, drained
lettuce leaves

Blend together the cream cheese and corn. Spread the mixture over each slice of ham. Place one asparagus spear on the edge of each ham slice and roll up. Chill, then cut each roll into 3.

Arrange lettuce on a serving platter and place the ham pinwheels on top.
Serves 6

EDAM AND HAM ROLLS
(Photograph: Dutch Dairy Bureau)

Cucumber and Gouda Appetizers

2 medium cucumbers
1 red-skinned apple, cored and
  chopped
4 oz. (1 cup) mushrooms, finely
  chopped
1 onion, finely chopped
4 oz. (1 cup) Gouda cheese, finely
  grated

1 teaspoon French mustard
4 tablespoons (¼ cup) mayonnaise
salt and freshly ground pepper
Garnish:
8 stuffed olives, sliced
parsley sprigs

Halve the cucumbers lengthways and scoop out the seeds. Cut each piece into 4. Plunge them into boiling water for 1 minute, drain and cool.

Place the apple, mushrooms, onion, cheese, mustard, mayonnaise, salt and pepper in a bowl and mix well. Pile the mixture into the cucumber shells and garnish with olive slices and parsley sprigs.

Serves 4

As a starter or party snack the above quantity will serve 8.

Grapefruit and Tuna Pâté

1 medium grapefruit
1 × 7 oz. can tuna
3 oz. (1½ cups) fresh white
  breadcrumbs
2 teaspoons grated onion
1 large egg, beaten
salt and freshly ground pepper

Garnish:
lettuce leaves
tomato wedges
twists of fresh grapefruit

Wash and dry the grapefruit then finely grate the peel. Cut the grapefruit in half and squeeze out the juice.

Place the tuna and liquid in a bowl and mash finely. Add the grapefruit peel, juice, breadcrumbs, onion and egg. Mix thoroughly and season to taste with salt and pepper.

Transfer to a greased 1 lb. loaf tin and smooth the top. Bake in a preheated moderate oven, 350°F, Gas Mark 4 for 40 minutes. Remove from the tin and leave to cool.

Serve cut into slices, garnished with lettuce, tomato wedges and grapefruit twists.

Serves 4–6

Chicken and Mushroom Pâté

1 lb. (2 cups) chicken livers
8 oz. (1 cup) lean pork, diced
8 oz. (12 slices) streaky (fatty)
  bacon, chopped
1 medium onion, sliced
½ teaspoon dried thyme
1 bay leaf
salt and freshly ground pepper
stock

8 oz. (2 cups) mushrooms
1-2 cloves garlic, crushed
1 oz. (2T) butter
¼ pint (⅔ cup) double (heavy)
  cream
2 eggs, beaten
1 teaspoon lemon juice
2 tablespoons vermouth
parsley sprigs to garnish

Clean the livers thoroughly and place in a pan with the pork, bacon and onion. Add the thyme, bay leaf, salt and pepper to taste, and enough stock to cover the ingredients. Cook over a gentle heat until all the meat is tender but not soft. Drain off the stock and allow the meats to cool. Remove the bay leaf.

Place the mixture in a blender and blend until the mixture is a fine paste. Add the mushrooms and garlic and blend for a few seconds more. Turn into a bowl and beat in the butter, cream, eggs and lemon juice. Heat the vermouth, set alight and add to the mixture.

Adjust the seasoning and turn the pâté into a 2 lb. loaf tin or pâté mould. Stand in a shallow meat tin half-filled with water and bake in a preheated moderate oven, 325°F, Gas Mark 3 for about 2 hours. Place a piece of aluminium foil on the surface and a weight on top, then allow to cool.

When cold, turn the pâté out of the tin, garnish with parsley sprigs and serve with crisp toast.
Serves 8

Egg and Prawn Mayonnaise

4 tablespoons (¼ cup) mayonnaise
¼ pint (⅔ cup) soured cream
1 teaspoon curry powder
6 hard-boiled eggs
4 oz. (⅔ cup) peeled prawns
  (shelled shrimp)

Garnish:
green pepper rings
onion rings

Blend together the mayonnaise, soured cream and curry powder. Chill for 1 hour. Cut the eggs in half and arrange them on a flat plate with the prawns (shrimp). Coat with the mayonnaise mixture and fill the centre with green pepper and onion rings.
Serves 4

Ham and Avocado Rolls

4 tomatoes, skinned and seeded
1 green or red pepper
1 stick celery, chopped
3 tablespoons mayonnaise
1 avocado

squeeze of lemon juice
salt and freshly ground pepper
8 large slices cooked ham
parsley sprigs to garnish

Cut the tomato flesh into strips. Place the pepper in boiling water for 5 minutes, drain, remove the seeds and pith and cut into strips. Reserve a few strips for the garnish. Place the tomatoes, pepper, celery and mayonnaise in a bowl and blend well together.

Remove the stone (pit) from the avocado, peel and cut the flesh into slices. Sprinkle with lemon juice and fold into the mayonnaise mixture, reserving a few slices for garnish. Season to taste with salt and pepper. Divide the mixture between the slices of ham and roll up.

Arrange on a plate and garnish with the reserved pepper strips, avocado slices and parsley sprigs.
Serves 4

Sweet and Savoury Pears

8 oz. (2 cups) Cheddar cheese, grated
2 red dessert apples, cored and chopped
2 oz. (½ cup) walnuts, chopped
2 oz. (⅓ cup) raisins
¼ pint (⅔ cup) milk

few drops of Worcestershire sauce
salt and freshly ground pepper
4 dessert pears
squeeze of lemon juice
Garnish:
lettuce leaves
tomato slices

Place the cheese, apples, walnuts, raisins and milk in a bowl and mix well. Add a few drops of Worcestershire sauce and salt and pepper to taste.

Cut the pears in half and remove the core. Sprinkle with a little lemon juice and pile the cheese and apple mixture on top of each pear half. Serve two halves per person, garnished with lettuce leaves and tomato slices.
Serves 4

HAM AND AVOCADO ROLLS
(Photograph: Carmel Produce Information Bureau)

Savoury Stuffed Tomatoes

6 rashers (slices) bacon, rinds
  removed and chopped
1 small onion, finely chopped
8 oz. (1 cup) cottage cheese with
  chives

salt and freshly ground pepper
½ pint (1 ¼ cups) (hard) cider
6 large tomatoes

Fry the bacon in a covered pan over a low heat until the fat begins to run. Add the onion and fry gently until soft. Drain off the excess fat and leave to cool.

Stir the bacon and onion into the cottage cheese and chives. Season to taste with salt and pepper. Boil the cider rapidly until it is reduced to 3 tablespoons then add to the cheese mixture.

Cut the tops from the tomatoes and remove the central core and seeds. Pile the cheese mixture into the shells, replace the lids and serve.
Serves 6

Samsoe Castles

1 lb. (4 cups) Samsoe cheese,
  coarsely grated

3 medium tomatoes, sliced

Place a slice of tomato in the bottom of four empty yogurt cartons (or similar containers). Divide half the grated cheese between the cartons, pressing down well. Place another slice of tomato over the cheese and top with the remaining cheese, again pressing firmly. Leave in a cool place to become firm.

To serve the castles, loosen them with a knife and turn out carefully onto a dish or individual plates. Serve with the remaining tomato slices and green salad.
Serves 4

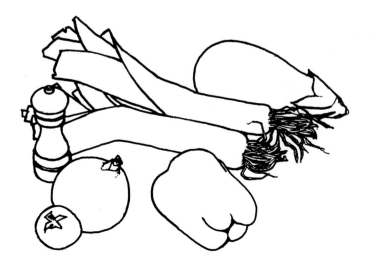

INDEX

INDEX